AF646353

Preface

Welcome to the world of English Olympiad MCQ With Solutions Class 12. We're thrilled to have you start this journey, which will open doors to new experiences, ideas, and connections. English is more than just a subject in school—it's a valuable skill that can enhance every part of your life, from making friends to exploring cultures, watching movies, and even navigating the internet. With English, you gain a tool to connect with people worldwide, express your thoughts clearly, and explore the richness of global literature, media, and knowledge.

This book is designed to make learning English enjoyable, practical, and comprehensive. Whether you're new to the language or have some experience, each chapter will guide you in mastering vocabulary, grammar, speaking, reading, writing, and listening skills. Through engaging stories, relatable characters, and fun activities, this book helps you see English in action and understand its power as a language of communication, creativity, and expression.

We follow the principles of the National Education Policy (NEP) 2020, which emphasises holistic, competency-based, and enjoyable learning. The NEP encourages practical skills, critical thinking, and meaningful engagement, and this book is designed to meet these goals. With every lesson, you'll build valuable competencies in academics and real-world situations. We've included activities and scenarios that bring English to life, from simple conversations to meaningful self-expression.

Additionally, we have integrated lessons that connect with the Sustainable Development Goals (SDGs), such as Quality Education, Gender Equality, Climate Action, and Peace and Justice. These goals encourage students to understand global challenges and work toward a better world. By learning English in this international context, you'll gain language skills and become more aware of how to contribute positively to the world.

As you read the book, remember that language learning is a gradual journey. Practice regularly, celebrate your progress, and enjoy the process. With each chapter, you'll discover the joy of expressing yourself, learning about new topics, and connecting with the world through English. We hope this book becomes a helpful companion in your journey. Happy learning!

Table of Contents

Chapter 1 - The Last Lesson (Alphonse Daudet)

Q1 Who is the author of "The Last Lesson"?
a. Victor Hugo
b. Alphonse Daudet
c. Marcel Proust
d. Émile Zola
Answer b. Alphonse Daudet

Q2 What is the setting of the story?
a. A city
b. A village in France
c. A school in America
d. A farm
Answer b. A village in France

Q3 Who is the protagonist of "The Last Lesson"?
a. M. Hamel
b. Franz
c. The narrator
d. Romain Rolland
Answer b. Franz

Q4 What does Franz feel on the last day of school?
a. Excitement
b. Happiness
c. Regret and sadness
d. Indifference
Answer c. Regret and sadness

Q5 Why is the last lesson significant?
a. It is a celebration
b. It marks the end of French lessons
c. It is an annual event
d. It introduces new subjects
Answer b. It marks the end of French lessons

Q6 Who teaches the last lesson?
a. The new teacher
b. M. Hamel
c. Franz's father
d. The village head
Answer b. M. Hamel

Q7 What does M. Hamel teach in the last lesson?
a. Mathematics
b. History
c. French language
d. Geography
Answer c. French language

Q8 What emotion does M. Hamel display during the lesson?
a. Anger
b. Pride
c. Sadness
d. Joy
Answer c. Sadness

Q9 How does Franz's perception of his teacher change throughout the story?
a. He grows to dislike him
b. He realizes his value
c. He becomes indifferent
d. He is always respectful
Answer b. He realizes his value

Q10 What does the story symbolize about education?
a. It is only about knowledge
b. It is valuable and should be cherished
c. It is unnecessary
d. It is temporary
Answer b. It is valuable and should be cherished

Q11 How does the village react to the announcement of the last lesson?
a. They are indifferent
b. They are supportive
c. They express regret
d. They celebrate
Answer c. They express regret

Q12 What does the phrase "The last lesson" signify in a broader context?
a. The end of learning
b. The end of an era
c. A new beginning
d. The importance of time
Answer b. The end of an era

Q13 What does Franz wish he had done before the last lesson?
a. Paid more attention
b. Studied harder
c. Left school earlier

d. Spoke to M. Hamel
Answer a. Paid more attention

Q14 The atmosphere in the classroom during the last lesson is
a. Joyful
b. Tense and solemn
c. Chaotic
d. Indifferent
Answer b. Tense and solemn

Q15 What does M. Hamel say about the French language?
a. It is useless
b. It is a symbol of freedom
c. It is too difficult
d. It is not important
Answer b. It is a symbol of freedom

Q16 How does the story depict the theme of patriotism?
a. Through the students' indifference
b. Through M. Hamel's passion for the language
c. Through Franz's lack of care
d. Through celebrations
Answer b. Through M. Hamel's passion for the language

Q17 What does Franz see when he looks out of the window during the lesson?
a. A beautiful garden
b. Soldiers marching
c. His friends playing
d. His father
Answer b. Soldiers marching

Q18 What does M. Hamel regret at the end of the lesson?
a. His lack of teaching experience
b. His decision to retire
c. Not teaching the students better
d. The state of the village
Answer c. Not teaching the students better

Q19 The last lesson evokes feelings of
a. Anger and frustration
b. Nostalgia and sorrow
c. Indifference
d. Joy
Answer b. Nostalgia and sorrow

Q20 What is the central message of "The Last Lesson"?
a. Education is irrelevant
b. Language is connected to identity and culture
c. School should be avoided
d. Teachers are unimportant
Answer b. Language is connected to identity and culture

Chapter 2 - Lost Spring (Anees Jung)

Q1 Who is the author of "Lost Spring"?
a. Ruskin Bond
b. Anees Jung
c. R. K. Narayan
d. Arundhati Roy
Answer b. Anees Jung

Q2 The story focuses on the lives of children working in
a. Factories
b. The streets
c. Glass-blowing and rag-picking
d. Schools
Answer c. Glass-blowing and rag-picking

Q3 Who is the first character introduced in the narrative?
a. Saheb
b. Shahid
c. The glass-blower
d. The narrator
Answer a. Saheb

Q4 What does Saheb's name mean?
a. Lord
b. Master
c. Helper
d. Child
Answer a. Lord

Q5 Saheb's family migrated to
a. Mumbai
b. Delhi
c. Kolkata
d. Bangalore
Answer b. Delhi

Q6 What are Saheb and his friends often seen doing?
a. Playing games
b. Selling newspapers
c. Searching for scraps
d. Going to school
Answer c. Searching for scraps

Q7 What is Saheb's dream?
a. To become a teacher
b. To own a shop
c. To go to America
d. To find a way out of poverty
Answer d. To find a way out of poverty

Q8 What does the narrator observe about the working conditions of the children?
a. They are happy
b. They are dangerous and exploitative
c. They are supportive
d. They are safe
Answer b. They are dangerous and exploitative

Q9 How does Saheb's attitude change throughout the story?
a. He becomes more hopeful
b. He becomes disheartened
c. He becomes more rebellious
d. He becomes indifferent
Answer b. He becomes disheartened

Q10 What does the story highlight about society's view on child labor?
a. It is acceptable
b. It is ignored
c. It is a serious issue that needs attention
d. It is celebrated
Answer c. It is a serious issue that needs attention

Q11 The second character introduced in the story is
a. A school teacher
b. A ragpicker
c. A glass-blower
d. A politician
Answer c. A glass-blower

Q12 What craft is associated with the glass-blower?
a. Making jewelry
b. Creating glass items
c. Repairing glass
d. Selling glass
Answer b. Creating glass items

Q13 The story reflects on the theme of
a. Freedom
b. Education and opportunity
c. Wealth and power

d. Family ties
Answer b. Education and opportunity

Q14 What does the glass-blower want for his children?
a. To continue his work
b. To get educated
c. To work with him
d. To migrate
Answer b. To get educated

Q15 The narrative emphasizes the harsh realities faced by
a. Children in poverty
b. Wealthy families
c. School children
d. Migrant workers
Answer a. Children in poverty

Q16 What does Saheb ultimately lose?
a. His job
b. His dreams
c. His family
d. His friends
Answer b. His dreams

Q17 The author uses descriptive imagery to highlight
a. The beauty of childhood
b. The harshness of life for the poor
c. The joy of childhood
d. The importance of education
Answer b. The harshness of life for the poor

Q18 The overall message of "Lost Spring" conveys that
a. Poverty is inevitable
b. Education is crucial for breaking the cycle of poverty
c. Child labor is acceptable
d. Children should be seen and not heard
Answer b. Education is crucial for breaking the cycle of poverty

Q19 How does the story portray the importance of dreams?
a. They are irrelevant
b. They motivate individuals to escape poverty
c. They are unattainable
d. They lead to disappointment
Answer b. They motivate individuals to escape poverty

Q20 The story concludes with a call to action for
a. The wealthy
b. Society to address child labor and education
c. Children to be quiet
d. Families to work harder
Answer b. Society to address child labor and education

Chapter 3 - Deep Water (William Douglas)

Q1 Who is the author of "Deep Water"?
a. Ernest Hemingway
b. William Douglas
c. Mark Twain
d. John Steinbeck
Answer b. William Douglas

Q2 The narrative focuses on the author's fear of
a. Heights
b. Water
c. Darkness
d. Animals
Answer b. Water

Q3 What incident in Douglas's childhood intensified his fear of water?
a. Drowning in a river
b. Falling off a boat
c. A near-drowning experience at a pool
d. Being pushed into a lake
Answer c. A near-drowning experience at a pool

Q4 How does the author describe his feelings toward water before the incident?
a. Love and excitement
b. Indifference
c. Fear and anxiety
d. Confidence
Answer c. Fear and anxiety

Q5 Who helps Douglas confront his fear of water?
a. His father
b. A swimming instructor
c. A friend
d. A therapist
Answer b. A swimming instructor

Q6 What technique does Douglas use to overcome his fear?
a. Avoiding water
b. Swimming lessons
c. Gradual exposure to water
d. Meditation
Answer c. Gradual exposure to water

Q7 The main setting of the story is
a. A lake
b. A swimming pool
c. An ocean
d. A river
Answer b. A swimming pool

Q8 What does Douglas do to prepare for his swimming lessons?
a. He studies swimming techniques
b. He avoids thinking about it
c. He practices diving
d. He runs away
Answer a. He studies swimming techniques

Q9 The author's experience with fear can be described as
a. Challenging but rewarding
b. Unnecessary
c. Common and unimportant
d. Irrelevant
Answer a. Challenging but rewarding

Q10 The story conveys the theme of
a. Avoidance of fears
b. Confronting and overcoming fears
c. The importance of swimming
d. The insignificance of water
Answer b. Confronting and overcoming fears

Q11 How does Douglas feel after learning to swim?
a. Disappointed
b. Confident and empowered
c. Indifferent
d. Scared
Answer b. Confident and empowered

Q12 What emotion does Douglas associate with water after overcoming his fear?
a. Joy
b. Sadness
c. Anger
d. Indifference
Answer a. Joy

Q13 What does the author's journey symbolize?
a. The importance of education
b. The journey from fear to confidence
c. The power of friendship

d. The need for safety
Answer b. The journey from fear to confidence

Q14 Douglas uses vivid imagery to describe
a. The beauty of nature
b. His fear of water
c. Swimming techniques
d. His childhood experiences
Answer b. His fear of water

Q15 The author emphasizes that overcoming fear requires
a. Time and effort
b. Natural talent
c. Support from friends
d. Wealth
Answer a. Time and effort

Q16 The conclusion of the story suggests that
a. Fear is inevitable
b. Fear can be conquered
c. Water is dangerous
d. Swimming is unnecessary
Answer b. Fear can be conquered

Q17 How does Douglas describe the feeling of learning to swim?
a. Like a burden
b. Like a joy
c. Like a failure
d. Like a distraction
Answer b. Like a joy

Q18 The story inspires readers to
a. Avoid challenges
b. Embrace their fears
c. Stay safe at all costs
d. Ignore their emotions
Answer b. Embrace their fears

Q19 What lesson does Douglas want to impart through his experience?
a. To avoid water
b. To confront one's fears
c. To rely on others
d. To give up
Answer b. To confront one's fears

Q20 The overall message of "Deep Water" reflects on
a. The dangers of water
b. The importance of facing one’s fears
c. The value of swimming lessons
d. The insignificance of childhood
Answer b. The importance of facing one’s fears

Chapter 4 - The Rattrap (Selma Lagerlof)

Q1 Who is the author of "The Rattrap"?
a. Selma Lagerlöf
b. Franz Kafka
c. Ernest Hemingway
d. Mark Twain
Answer a. Selma Lagerlöf

Q2 The protagonist of the story is
a. A wealthy merchant
b. A poor vagabond
c. A king
d. A farmer
Answer b. A poor vagabond

Q3 What does the vagabond sell to earn money?
a. Rattraps
b. Food
c. Clothes
d. Tools
Answer a. Rattraps

Q4 The vagabond's view of the world can be described as
a. Optimistic
b. Pessimistic
c. Indifferent
d. Joyful
Answer b. Pessimistic

Q5 What metaphor is used to describe life in the story?
a. A journey
b. A game
c. A rattrap
d. A race
Answer c. A rattrap

Q6 What is the main theme of "The Rattrap"?
a. The futility of life
b. The importance of friendship
c. The concept of compassion and redemption
d. The power of wealth
Answer c. The concept of compassion and redemption

Q7 How does the vagabond end up at the old man's house?
a. He is lost
b. He is invited
c. He is escaping from the police
d. He is seeking shelter
Answer d. He is seeking shelter

Q8 The old man who takes in the vagabond is characterized as
a. Suspicious
b. Generous and kind
c. Indifferent
d. Greedy
Answer b. Generous and kind

Q9 What does the old man share with the vagabond during their conversation?
a. His wealth
b. His food
c. His stories and experiences
d. His business secrets
Answer c. His stories and experiences

Q10 How does the vagabond react to the old man's kindness?
a. He is indifferent
b. He feels guilty
c. He is angry
d. He is grateful
Answer d. He is grateful

Q11 The vagabond steals money from the old man, which signifies
a. Desperation
b. Greed
c. The end of friendship
d. Regret
Answer a. Desperation

Q12 What does the vagabond realize after stealing from the old man?
a. His actions have consequences
b. He can escape easily
c. He is stronger than he thought
d. Money is more important
Answer a. His actions have consequences

Q13 The rattrap symbolizes
a. Wealth and luxury
b. Life's entrapments and struggles
c. Freedom

d. Joy and happiness
Answer b. Life's entrapments and struggles

Q14 What change occurs in the vagabond by the end of the story?
a. He becomes richer
b. He learns to appreciate kindness
c. He remains unchanged
d. He leaves the old man forever
Answer b. He learns to appreciate kindness

Q15 The climax of the story involves
a. The vagabond's escape
b. The old man's realization
c. The vagabond's decision to return the money
d. A fight between the characters
Answer c. The vagabond's decision to return the money

Q16 What does the story ultimately convey about human nature?
a. It is inherently selfish
b. It is capable of change and compassion
c. It is untrustworthy
d. It is indifferent
Answer b. It is capable of change and compassion

Q17 The story reflects on the importance of
a. Wealth and status
b. Friendship and generosity
c. Adventure and excitement
d. Education
Answer b. Friendship and generosity

Q18 How does the author portray the vagabond's character throughout the story?
a. As a villain
b. As a complex individual with flaws
c. As a hero
d. As a coward
Answer b. As a complex individual with flaws

Q19 What role does the setting play in the story?
a. It adds to the complexity of characters
b. It is irrelevant to the plot
c. It emphasizes the vagabond's isolation
d. It highlights wealth
Answer c. It emphasizes the vagabond's isolation

Q20 The overall message of "The Rattrap" emphasizes
a. The futility of life
b. The importance of human connections and redemption
c. The insignificance of poverty
d. The necessity of wealth
Answer b. The importance of human connections and redemption

Chapter 5 - Indigo (Louis Fischer)

Q1 Who is the author of "Indigo"?
a. R. K. Narayan
b. Louis Fischer
c. M. K. Gandhi
d. B. R. Ambedkar
Answer b. Louis Fischer

Q2 The story primarily focuses on
a. The cotton industry
b. The struggle for indigo farmers
c. The fight for freedom
d. The history of textiles
Answer b. The struggle for indigo farmers

Q3 What is the main cause of the farmers' distress in the story?
a. Drought
b. Debt and exploitation by the British
c. Lack of education
d. Natural disasters
Answer b. Debt and exploitation by the British

Q4 Who plays a significant role in the indigo farmers' struggle?
a. A local leader
b. Louis Fischer
c. Mahatma Gandhi
d. A British official
Answer c. Mahatma Gandhi

Q5 How does Gandhi contribute to the indigo farmers' cause?
a. By organizing protests
b. By ignoring them
c. By offering financial support
d. By working with the British
Answer a. By organizing protests

Q6 The indigo farmers are exploited through
a. High prices for indigo
b. Land leases
c. Forceful cultivation of indigo
d. Lack of support from the government
Answer c. Forceful cultivation of indigo

Q7 What does the title "Indigo" symbolize in the story?
a. Wealth
b. Freedom and resistance
c. Tradition
d. Agriculture
Answer b. Freedom and resistance

Q8 What was the response of the British planters to the farmers' complaints?
a. They listened and made changes
b. They ignored the farmers
c. They supported the farmers
d. They increased prices
Answer b. They ignored the farmers

Q9 The indigo farmers' situation reflects the broader theme of
a. Economic exploitation
b. Industrial growth
c. Urbanization
d. Cultural preservation
Answer a. Economic exploitation

Q10 What method did Gandhi use to protest against the exploitation?
a. Violence
b. Non-violent civil disobedience
c. Legal action
d. Political negotiation
Answer b. Non-violent civil disobedience

Q11 The story illustrates the impact of colonialism on
a. Indian agriculture
b. British industries
c. Urban development
d. International trade
Answer a. Indian agriculture

Q12 How does Gandhi inspire the farmers?
a. By promising wealth
b. By encouraging them to fight back
c. By showing them the power of unity and non-violence
d. By providing them with weapons
Answer c. By showing them the power of unity and non-violence

Q13 What is the ultimate goal of the indigo farmers' struggle?
a. To gain land
b. To seek justice and fair treatment
c. To become wealthy

d. To migrate
Answer b. To seek justice and fair treatment

Q14 What role does the concept of non-violence play in the story?
a. It is disregarded
b. It is central to the farmers' struggle
c. It is a hindrance
d. It is unimportant
Answer b. It is central to the farmers' struggle

Q15 The outcome of the farmers' struggle demonstrates the power of
a. Wealth
b. Unity and solidarity
c. Political influence
d. Education
Answer b. Unity and solidarity

Q16 How does the story "Indigo" conclude?
a. With despair
b. With hope and empowerment
c. With continued oppression
d. With a return to old practices
Answer b. With hope and empowerment

Q17 The author uses vivid imagery to depict
a. The beauty of indigo plants
b. The harsh realities of farming life
c. The wealth of the planters
d. The simplicity of village life
Answer b. The harsh realities of farming life

Q18 The story emphasizes the importance of
a. Wealth
b. Community and collaboration
c. Individual success
d. Competition
Answer b. Community and collaboration

Q19 What does the author reveal about the impact of colonialism on culture?
a. It enriches culture
b. It destroys traditions
c. It has no impact
d. It promotes cultural exchange
Answer b. It destroys traditions

Q20 The overall message of "Indigo" reflects on
a. The need for industrialization
b. The significance of resistance and hope in the face of oppression
c. The value of traditional practices
d. The importance of wealth accumulation
Answer b. The significance of resistance and hope in the face of oppression

Chapter 6 - Poets and Pancakes

Q1 Who is the author of "Poets and Pancakes"?
a. R. K. Narayan
b. A. P. J. Abdul Kalam
c. A. P. J. Abdul Kalam
d. A. J. Cronin
Answer a. R. K. Narayan

Q2 What is the main focus of the narrative?
a. The life of a poet
b. The significance of pancakes
c. The author's experiences in the film industry
d. The importance of education
Answer c. The author's experiences in the film industry

Q3 The story is set in which city?
a. Mumbai
b. Chennai
c. Kolkata
d. Bangalore
Answer b. Chennai

Q4 The author recounts his experiences working for a
a. Newspaper
b. Film studio
c. Radio station
d. Theatre
Answer b. Film studio

Q5 The title "Poets and Pancakes" symbolizes the
a. Contrast between art and daily life
b. Importance of breakfast
c. Relationship between different professions
d. Value of tradition
Answer a. Contrast between art and daily life

Q6 Who is the character that represents the film industry?
a. A writer
b. A director
c. A producer
d. A poet
Answer d. A poet

Q7 The author describes the poet as being
a. Successful and wealthy
b. Humorous and carefree
c. Struggling and disheartened
d. Angry and rebellious
Answer c. Struggling and disheartened

Q8 The interactions in the film studio highlight the theme of
a. Creativity
b. Competition
c. Friendship
d. Pretension
Answer d. Pretension

Q9 What does the poet's struggle reflect about the nature of art?
a. It is easy to achieve
b. It is often undervalued
c. It is solely for entertainment
d. It is important for society
Answer b. It is often undervalued

Q10 How does the author describe the pancakes?
a. Delicious and comforting
b. Unappetizing
c. Overrated
d. Complicated to make
Answer a. Delicious and comforting

Q11 The narrative reveals the complexity of
a. Fame
b. Relationships
c. Artistic expression
d. Financial success
Answer c. Artistic expression

Q12 The author's observations about the poet serve to illustrate
a. The importance of breakfast
b. The difficulties faced by artists
c. The joy of life
d. The need for education
Answer b. The difficulties faced by artists

Q13 What does the story ultimately suggest about poets?
a. They are not respected
b. They lead glamorous lives
c. They are misunderstood and undervalued

d. They are always successful
Answer c. They are misunderstood and undervalued

Q14 The tone of the narrative can be described as
a. Serious and somber
b. Light-hearted and humorous
c. Indifferent
d. Angry
Answer b. Light-hearted and humorous

Q15 The author's experiences in the film industry reveal the contrast between
a. Reality and illusion
b. Wealth and poverty
c. Knowledge and ignorance
d. Tradition and modernity
Answer a. Reality and illusion

Q16 What does the author's interaction with the poet signify?
a. The bond between artists
b. The competition in art
c. The loneliness of creativity
d. The insignificance of their work
Answer c. The loneliness of creativity

Q17 The relationship between food and creativity is portrayed as
a. Unrelated
b. Vital for inspiration
c. Distracting
d. Overrated
Answer b. Vital for inspiration

Q18 The narrative emphasizes the importance of
a. Material success
b. Supportive relationships
c. Independence
d. Competition
Answer b. Supportive relationships

Q19 How does the story challenge stereotypes about artists?
a. By portraying them as wealthy
b. By showing their struggles and complexities
c. By ignoring their work
d. By celebrating their success
Answer b. By showing their struggles and complexities

Q20 The overall message of "Poets and Pancakes" reflects on
a. The pursuit of material wealth
b. The challenges faced by artists and the importance of creativity
c. The joy of cooking
d. The need for education
Answer b. The challenges faced by artists and the importance of creativity

Chapter 7 - The Interview

Q1 Who is the author of "The Interview"?
a. James Thurber
b. R. K. Narayan
c. J. B. Priestley
d. A. P. J. Abdul Kalam
Answer a. James Thurber

Q2 The story revolves around
a. A job interview
b. A marriage interview
c. A college admission interview
d. A media interview
Answer a. A job interview

Q3 What is the protagonist's name?
a. Mr. Smith
b. Mr. Jones
c. Mr. Brown
d. Mr. Davis
Answer a. Mr. Smith

Q4 What is the setting of the interview?
a. An office
b. A café
c. A home
d. A university
Answer a. An office

Q5 How does the protagonist feel before the interview?
a. Calm and confident
b. Nervous and anxious
c. Indifferent
d. Excited
Answer b. Nervous and anxious

Q6 What does the interviewer primarily focus on during the interview?
a. The applicant's education
b. The applicant's appearance
c. The applicant's personality and character
d. The applicant's salary expectations
Answer c. The applicant's personality and character

Q7 What type of questions does the interviewer ask?
a. Personal and irrelevant
b. Professional and direct
c. Easy and casual
d. Difficult and complex
Answer b. Professional and direct

Q8 The protagonist's responses during the interview reveal
a. His lack of experience
b. His nervousness and insecurity
c. His confidence
d. His disinterest
Answer b. His nervousness and insecurity

Q9 How does the interviewer perceive the protagonist?
a. As competent and skilled
b. As unqualified
c. As charming and engaging
d. As rude
Answer c. As charming and engaging

Q10 What does the story ultimately suggest about interviews?
a. They are always stressful
b. They reflect the true abilities of individuals
c. They can be subjective and influenced by personality
d. They are irrelevant
Answer c. They can be subjective and influenced by personality

Q11 The protagonist's experiences in the interview highlight the importance of
a. Academic qualifications
b. Presentation and personality
c. Professional attire
d. Networking
Answer b. Presentation and personality

Q12 What lesson does the protagonist learn by the end of the interview?
a. To avoid interviews
b. To prepare better
c. To be himself
d. To dress well
Answer c. To be himself

Q13 The tone of the narrative can be described as
a. Serious
b. Humorous and light-hearted
c. Sad

d. Angry
Answer b. Humorous and light-hearted

Q14 The story reflects on the theme of
a. Competition
b. Opportunity
c. Self-awareness
d. Hard work
Answer c. Self-awareness

Q15 How does the story portray the role of interviews in job selection?
a. They are crucial
b. They are unimportant
c. They are a mere formality
d. They are unnecessary
Answer a. They are crucial

Q16 What does the protagonist hope to achieve through the interview?
a. A job offer
b. Networking opportunities
c. Experience
d. A chance to meet new people
Answer a. A job offer

Q17 The protagonist's self-reflection after the interview emphasizes the need for
a. Professional development
b. Self-confidence
c. Education
d. Experience
Answer b. Self-confidence

Q18 The overall message of "The Interview" conveys that
a. Interviews are daunting
b. They reflect personal growth and character
c. Success is only about qualifications
d. Networking is key
Answer b. They reflect personal growth and character

Q19 The author uses humor to illustrate
a. The absurdity of job hunting
b. The ease of interviews
c. The seriousness of employment
d. The importance of research
Answer a. The absurdity of job hunting

Q20 The protagonist's journey through the interview process highlights the value of
a. Preparation
b. Family connections
c. Personal appearance
d. Intimidation
Answer a. Preparation

Chapter 8 - Going Places (A. R. Barton)

Q1 Who is the author of "Going Places"?
a. R. K. Narayan
b. A. R. Barton
c. Anton Chekhov
d. Jane Austen
Answer b. A. R. Barton

Q2 The story revolves around the character of
a. A young girl named Sophie
b. A boy named Paul
c. A man named Max
d. A woman named Clara
Answer a. A young girl named Sophie

Q3 Sophie dreams of
a. Traveling the world
b. Becoming a fashion designer
c. Owning a shop
d. Marrying a wealthy man
Answer a. Traveling the world

Q4 How does Sophie perceive her family's financial situation?
a. She is indifferent
b. She is embarrassed
c. She is proud
d. She is frustrated
Answer b. She is embarrassed

Q5 What does Sophie fantasize about?
a. Being a model
b. Having a luxurious life
c. Marrying a film star
d. Traveling to Paris
Answer d. Traveling to Paris

Q6 How does Sophie feel about her school life?
a. Excited
b. Boring
c. Adventurous
d. Unhappy
Answer d. Unhappy

Q7 The character of Sophie is characterized by
a. Indifference
b. Ambition and dreams
c. A lack of imagination
d. Resentment
Answer b. Ambition and dreams

Q8 Sophie often daydreams about
a. Her friends
b. Her future
c. Her enemies
d. Her teachers
Answer b. Her future

Q9 How does Sophie's family react to her dreams?
a. They encourage her
b. They ridicule her
c. They ignore her
d. They support her
Answer b. They ridicule her

Q10 The story highlights the theme of
a. Reality versus dreams
b. Wealth
c. Family relationships
d. Education
Answer a. Reality versus dreams

Q11 What does Sophie's imagination reveal about her character?
a. She is unrealistic
b. She is practical
c. She is adventurous and hopeful
d. She is irresponsible
Answer c. She is adventurous and hopeful

Q12 The ending of the story can be described as
a. Happy and fulfilling
b. Open-ended and ambiguous
c. Sad and disappointing
d. Clear and concise
Answer b. Open-ended and ambiguous

Q13 How does Sophie's story reflect the struggles of youth?
a. It highlights their carefree nature
b. It shows their desire for independence and dreams
c. It dismisses their ambitions

d. It celebrates their ignorance
Answer b. It shows their desire for independence and dreams

Q14 What do Sophie's daydreams symbolize?
a. A lack of maturity
b. Hope and aspirations
c. Naivety
d. Futility
Answer b. Hope and aspirations

Q15 The story conveys a message about
a. The need for realism
b. The value of dreaming big
c. The importance of education
d. The necessity of wealth
Answer b. The value of dreaming big

Q16 Sophie's interactions with her peers are characterized by
a. Hostility
b. Support
c. Indifference
d. Competition
Answer c. Indifference

Q17 The author uses vivid descriptions to illustrate
a. Sophie's environment
b. Sophie's emotions
c. The setting
d. The other characters
Answer b. Sophie's emotions

Q18 The overall tone of "Going Places" can be described as
a. Cheerful
b. Somber
c. Reflective and dreamy
d. Angry
Answer c. Reflective and dreamy

Q19 What lesson does the story impart about dreams?
a. They are unattainable
b. They can lead to disappointment
c. They are important for personal growth
d. They should be abandoned
Answer c. They are important for personal growth

Q20 Sophie's character can be seen as a representation of
a. The limitations of youth
b. The spirit of adventure
c. The importance of family
d. The futility of dreams
Answer b. The spirit of adventure

Chapter 9 - My Mother at Sixty-Six (Kamala Das)

Q1 Who is the author of the poem "My Mother at Sixty-Six"?
a. Kamala Das
b. Maya Angelou
c. Sarojini Naidu
d. Elizabeth Bishop
Answer a. Kamala Das

Q2 What is the central theme of the poem?
a. The beauty of youth
b. The inevitability of aging and loss
c. The joy of motherhood
d. The struggles of life
Answer b. The inevitability of aging and loss

Q3 How does the poet describe her mother in the poem?
a. As vibrant and youthful
b. As old and frail
c. As happy and cheerful
d. As busy and indifferent
Answer b. As old and frail

Q4 The poet's feelings towards her mother can be described as
a. Indifferent
b. Joyful
c. Sad and reflective
d. Angry
Answer c. Sad and reflective

Q5 What does the poet see in her mother's face?
a. Happiness
b. Anger
c. Sorrow and wrinkles
d. Youthfulness
Answer c. Sorrow and wrinkles

Q6 The journey mentioned in the poem represents
a. The journey of life
b. A physical trip
c. A spiritual journey
d. A quest for knowledge
Answer a. The journey of life

Q7 How does the poet feel about her mother's aging?
a. Proud
b. Fearful
c. Indifferent
d. Happy
Answer b. Fearful

Q8 What imagery does Kamala Das use to depict her mother's frailty?
a. Bright colors
b. Dark shadows
c. A smile
d. The road
Answer b. Dark shadows

Q9 The repetition of "my mother" emphasizes
a. Love and attachment
b. Indifference
c. Anger
d. Regret
Answer a. Love and attachment

Q10 The poem evokes feelings of
a. Joy and celebration
b. Nostalgia and sorrow
c. Indifference
d. Anger
Answer b. Nostalgia and sorrow

Q11 What is the poet's attitude towards her mother's condition?
a. Disregard
b. Acceptance
c. Sorrowful
d. Joyful
Answer c. Sorrowful

Q12 How does the poet feel as she leaves her mother?
a. Happy
b. Relieved
c. Sad and apprehensive
d. Indifferent
Answer c. Sad and apprehensive

Q13 The overall tone of the poem can be described as
a. Light-hearted
b. Melancholic
c. Joyful

d. Angry
Answer b. Melancholic

Q14 What does the imagery of the "road" symbolize in the poem?
a. Journey of life
b. The poet's childhood
c. Freedom
d. Chaos
Answer a. Journey of life

Q15 What does the poet compare her mother to in the poem?
a. A flower
b. A tree
c. A bird
d. A shadow
Answer d. A shadow

Q16 The theme of familial love is expressed through
a. Anger
b. Sorrow
c. Indifference
d. Joy
Answer b. Sorrow

Q17 The poet's perspective on aging reflects
a. Acceptance
b. Fear and sadness
c. Indifference
d. Happiness
Answer b. Fear and sadness

Q18 What emotion dominates the poem?
a. Joy
b. Regret
c. Sorrow
d. Anger
Answer c. Sorrow

Q19 The last lines of the poem suggest
a. Hope
b. Despair
c. Acceptance of reality
d. Denial
Answer c. Acceptance of reality

Q20 "My Mother at Sixty-Six" ultimately reflects on the relationship between
a. Life and death
b. Mother and child
c. Man and nature
d. Past and future
Answer b. Mother and child

Chapter 10 - An Elementary School Classroom in a Slum (Stephen Spender)

Q1 Who is the author of "An Elementary School Classroom in a Slum"?
a. Stephen Spender
b. John Keats
c. William Wordsworth
d. T. S. Eliot
Answer a. Stephen Spender

Q2 The poem highlights the conditions of children in
a. Rich neighborhoods
b. Urban slums
c. Rural areas
d. Private schools
Answer b. Urban slums

Q3 The children in the classroom are characterized by
a. Wealth and privilege
b. Happiness and joy
c. Poverty and neglect
d. Knowledge and curiosity
Answer c. Poverty and neglect

Q4 What does the poet compare the children's faces to?
a. Bright flowers
b. Darkened skies
c. Smiling faces
d. Shining stars
Answer b. Darkened skies

Q5 The imagery in the poem emphasizes
a. The beauty of nature
b. The harsh realities of life
c. The joy of childhood
d. The importance of education
Answer b. The harsh realities of life

Q6 The poet expresses a desire for the children to
a. Forget their troubles
b. Receive better education and opportunities
c. Leave the slum
d. Play outside
Answer b. Receive better education and opportunities

Q7 The classroom is described as
a. Well-lit and cheerful
b. Dark and gloomy
c. Modern and clean
d. Noisy and chaotic
Answer b. Dark and gloomy

Q8 What does the poet suggest about the education system?
a. It is effective for everyone
b. It fails to address the needs of the poor
c. It is perfect
d. It is irrelevant
Answer b. It fails to address the needs of the poor

Q9 The children in the poem are depicted as
a. Happy and content
b. Sad and hopeless
c. Independent and free
d. Joyful and curious
Answer b. Sad and hopeless

Q10 The poet uses vivid imagery to illustrate the children's
a. Dreams and aspirations
b. Suffering and despair
c. Adventures and fun
d. Talents and abilities
Answer b. Suffering and despair

Q11 The phrase "The stunted trees" refers to
a. The school building
b. The children's limited growth and potential
c. Nature
d. The environment
Answer b. The children's limited growth and potential

Q12 What does the poem suggest about society's view of slum children?
a. They are valued
b. They are ignored
c. They are celebrated
d. They are empowered
Answer b. They are ignored

Q13 The poet's tone can be described as
a. Joyful
b. Critical and empathetic
c. Indifferent

d. Angry
Answer b. Critical and empathetic

Q14 The ending of the poem leaves readers with a sense of
a. Hope and joy
b. Despair and concern
c. Indifference
d. Satisfaction
Answer b. Despair and concern

Q15 The poet's message emphasizes the importance of
a. Material wealth
b. Education and equality
c. Individual success
d. Isolation
Answer b. Education and equality

Q16 The overall theme of the poem is centered around
a. The beauty of childhood
b. The struggles of the marginalized in society
c. The importance of wealth
d. The joy of learning
Answer b. The struggles of the marginalized in society

Q17 The children's aspirations are depicted as
a. Bright and hopeful
b. Achievable
c. Limited and stifled
d. Non-existent
Answer c. Limited and stifled

Q18 The poem reflects on the harsh realities faced by
a. Teachers
b. The rich
c. Slum children
d. The elderly
Answer c. Slum children

Q19 The author uses powerful imagery to evoke feelings of
a. Happiness
b. Sympathy and awareness
c. Anger
d. Fear
Answer b. Sympathy and awareness

Q20 The overall message of "An Elementary School Classroom in a Slum" is about
a. The need for societal change to support underprivileged children
b. The irrelevance of education
c. The joy of childhood
d. The importance of wealth
Answer a. The need for societal change to support underprivileged children

Chapter 11 - Keeping Quiet (Pablo Neruda)

Q1 Who is the author of "Keeping Quiet"?
a. Pablo Neruda
b. Gabriel García Márquez
c. Jorge Luis Borges
d. Octavio Paz
Answer a. Pablo Neruda

Q2 The central theme of the poem revolves around
a. Peace and tranquility
b. War and conflict
c. Silence and introspection
d. Love and relationships
Answer c. Silence and introspection

Q3 What does the poet suggest about silence?
a. It is unnecessary
b. It is an opportunity for reflection
c. It is dull
d. It is a sign of weakness
Answer b. It is an opportunity for reflection

Q4 What action does the poet propose to undertake?
a. To fight
b. To speak out
c. To keep quiet
d. To leave
Answer c. To keep quiet

Q5 How does Neruda view the concept of action?
a. As always positive
b. As sometimes destructive
c. As irrelevant
d. As always necessary
Answer b. As sometimes destructive

Q6 The imagery in the poem often reflects
a. The beauty of nature
b. The chaos of society
c. The tranquility of silence
d. The complexity of human emotions
Answer c. The tranquility of silence

Q7 The poet emphasizes the importance of
a. Violence
b. Listening and understanding
c. Individualism
d. Competition
Answer b. Listening and understanding

Q8 What does the poet hope to achieve through silence?
a. Revenge
b. Reflection and awareness
c. Indifference
d. Noise
Answer b. Reflection and awareness

Q9 The phrase "to be still" in the poem suggests
a. Inaction
b. Contemplation
c. Fear
d. Weakness
Answer b. Contemplation

Q10 What does Neruda imply about human nature in the poem?
a. It is peaceful
b. It is destructive
c. It is indifferent
d. It is always good
Answer b. It is destructive

Q11 The overall tone of the poem can be described as
a. Angry
b. Reflective and contemplative
c. Joyful
d. Indifferent
Answer b. Reflective and contemplative

Q12 The poet's call for silence is ultimately a plea for
a. Ignorance
b. Awareness and understanding
c. Confrontation
d. Wealth
Answer b. Awareness and understanding

Q13 How does Neruda envision a world that embraces silence?
a. Chaotic
b. Peaceful and harmonious
c. Indifferent

d. Fearful
Answer b. Peaceful and harmonious

Q14 The poet uses the concept of keeping quiet to critique
a. Society's values
b. Personal success
c. Educational systems
d. Political ideologies
Answer a. Society's values

Q15 What does the poem encourage readers to reflect upon?
a. Their material possessions
b. The importance of action
c. Their inner thoughts and feelings
d. Their societal roles
Answer c. Their inner thoughts and feelings

Q16 The overall message of "Keeping Quiet" emphasizes
a. The futility of peace
b. The necessity of quiet reflection
c. The importance of action
d. The significance of wealth
Answer b. The necessity of quiet reflection

Q17 The poem reflects a desire for
a. Indifference
b. Global unity and peace
c. Conflict
d. Competition
Answer b. Global unity and peace

Q18 The theme of interconnectedness is expressed through
a. Individual experiences
b. Shared silence and reflection
c. Personal ambitions
d. Material pursuits
Answer b. Shared silence and reflection

Q19 How does Neruda portray the relationship between silence and understanding?
a. They are unrelated
b. Silence leads to deeper understanding
c. Understanding comes from noise
d. Silence is useless
Answer b. Silence leads to deeper understanding

Q20 The poem "Keeping Quiet" ultimately advocates for

a. Active protest

b. Thoughtful silence

c. Indifference to issues

d. Constant activity

Answer b. Thoughtful silence

Chapter 12 - A Thing of Beauty (John Keats)

Q1 Who is the author of "A Thing of Beauty"?
a. William Wordsworth
b. John Keats
c. Lord Byron
d. Samuel Taylor Coleridge
Answer b. John Keats

Q2 The central theme of the poem is
a. The importance of wealth
b. The beauty of nature and its impact on the soul
c. The value of friendship
d. The struggles of life
Answer b. The beauty of nature and its impact on the soul

Q3 What does Keats describe as a "thing of beauty"?
a. A person
b. Nature
c. Art
d. A moment in time
Answer b. Nature

Q4 According to Keats, beauty brings
a. Joy and happiness
b. Sadness and despair
c. Anger and resentment
d. Indifference
Answer a. Joy and happiness

Q5 The poem suggests that beauty has the power to
a. Heal the world
b. Inspire and uplift the human spirit
c. Cause pain
d. Create conflict
Answer b. Inspire and uplift the human spirit

Q6 The phrase "a thing of beauty" represents
a. Material possessions
b. Transitory moments
c. Eternal and lasting beauty
d. Seasonal changes
Answer c. Eternal and lasting beauty

Q7 What does Keats believe beauty can do for humanity?
a. Create conflict
b. Provide solace and comfort
c. Lead to despair
d. Generate wealth
Answer b. Provide solace and comfort

Q8 The imagery in the poem focuses on
a. Urban life
b. Natural elements
c. Industrialization
d. Human relationships
Answer b. Natural elements

Q9 How does Keats describe the effects of beauty on the soul?
a. It dulls the senses
b. It nourishes and enriches
c. It is irrelevant
d. It causes confusion
Answer b. It nourishes and enriches

Q10 The poem evokes feelings of
a. Anger
b. Peace and serenity
c. Frustration
d. Sadness
Answer b. Peace and serenity

Q11 What does the poet suggest about the relationship between beauty and nature?
a. They are unrelated
b. Beauty is fleeting
c. Nature is the source of beauty
d. Nature is indifferent to beauty
Answer c. Nature is the source of beauty

Q12 The line "and such are daffodils" refers to
a. The beauty of flowers
b. The transience of life
c. The importance of growth
d. The joy of spring
Answer a. The beauty of flowers

Q13 How does Keats convey the permanence of beauty?
a. Through seasonal changes
b. By referring to nature's cyclical patterns
c. Through the human experience

d. By emphasizing memories
**Answer b. By referring to nature's cyclical patterns

Q14 The poet's tone can be described as
a. Somber
b. Joyful and celebratory
c. Indifferent
d. Angry
Answer b. Joyful and celebratory

Q15 What does the phrase "grandeur of the sun" symbolize?
a. Wealth
b. Power and strength
c. Natural beauty and inspiration
d. Indifference
Answer c. Natural beauty and inspiration

Q16 The overall message of "A Thing of Beauty" suggests that
a. Beauty is temporary
b. Nature is a source of everlasting beauty
c. Life is filled with sorrow
d. Wealth is necessary for happiness
Answer b. Nature is a source of everlasting beauty

Q17 The poem reflects on the idea that beauty can
a. Bring pain
b. Inspire creativity and positivity
c. Lead to loss
d. Create conflict
Answer b. Inspire creativity and positivity

Q18 What does Keats use to illustrate the impact of beauty on the human experience?
a. Personal anecdotes
b. Nature imagery
c. Historical references
d. Urban landscapes
Answer b. Nature imagery

Q19 The conclusion of the poem emphasizes the importance of
a. Understanding beauty
b. Ignoring the natural world
c. Pursuing wealth
d. Competing with others
Answer a. Understanding beauty

Q20 "A Thing of Beauty" ultimately conveys a message about
a. The insignificance of beauty
b. The enduring power of beauty in life
c. The futility of existence
d. The importance of wealth
Answer b. The enduring power of beauty in life

Chapter 13 - A Roadside Stand

Q1 Who is the author of "A Roadside Stand"?
a. Robert Frost
b. Walt Whitman
c. Emily Dickinson
d. John Keats
Answer a. Robert Frost

Q2 The poem depicts the struggles of
a. Urban dwellers
b. Farmers
c. Children
d. Businessmen
Answer b. Farmers

Q3 What is the setting of the poem?
a. A busy city
b. A rural roadside
c. A bustling market
d. A schoolyard
Answer b. A rural roadside

Q4 The roadside stand represents
a. Prosperity
b. The hopes and dreams of rural people
c. Indifference
d. Isolation
Answer b. The hopes and dreams of rural people

Q5 The poem reflects on the theme of
a. Urban development
b. Nature
c. Poverty and social inequality
d. Individual success
Answer c. Poverty and social inequality

Q6 What do the farmers hope to gain from their roadside stand?
a. Wealth
b. Recognition
c. A sense of community
d. Financial stability
Answer d. Financial stability

Q7 The poet expresses concern about
a. The destruction of nature
b. The neglect of rural communities
c. The rise of technology
d. The beauty of life
Answer b. The neglect of rural communities

Q8 How does the poet describe the response of passersby to the stand?
a. They are curious
b. They are indifferent
c. They are supportive
d. They are critical
Answer b. They are indifferent

Q9 The phrase "the people" in the poem symbolizes
a. Urban dwellers
b. Those in power
c. The working class
d. The wealthy
Answer c. The working class

Q10 What does the poet imply about the dreams of the farmers?
a. They are unattainable
b. They are irrelevant
c. They are crucial for survival
d. They are easily achieved
Answer c. They are crucial for survival

Q11 The overall tone of the poem can be described as
a. Joyful
b. Melancholic and reflective
c. Angry
d. Indifferent
Answer b. Melancholic and reflective

Q12 What does the author hope for the future of rural communities?
a. Urbanization
b. Prosperity and recognition
c. Isolation
d. Destruction
Answer b. Prosperity and recognition

Q13 The poem highlights the importance of
a. Individual success
b. Community support
c. Technology

d. Wealth accumulation
Answer b. Community support

Q14 What is the significance of the roadside stand in the poem?
a. It symbolizes wealth
b. It represents dreams and aspirations
c. It is irrelevant
d. It is a source of entertainment
Answer b. It represents dreams and aspirations

Q15 The author's use of imagery emphasizes
a. Urban life
b. Nature's beauty
c. The struggles of rural existence
d. The joy of childhood
Answer c. The struggles of rural existence

Q16 The ending of the poem suggests that
a. Change is inevitable
b. Rural dreams are fading
c. Hope remains alive
d. Wealth is paramount
Answer c. Hope remains alive

Q17 How does the poet convey a sense of community in the poem?
a. Through individual stories
b. Through shared struggles and dreams
c. Through celebration
d. Through wealth
Answer b. Through shared struggles and dreams

Q18 The poem encourages readers to reflect on
a. The importance of wealth
b. The value of community and connection
c. The futility of rural life
d. The joys of urban living
Answer b. The value of community and connection

Q19 What does the poet hope for the farmers' future?
a. More hardships
b. Increased wealth
c. Recognition and success
d. Urban relocation
Answer c. Recognition and success

Q20 "A Roadside Stand" ultimately conveys a message about
a. The beauty of nature
b. The significance of dreams and community
c. The importance of individualism
d. The joy of competition
Answer b. The significance of dreams and community

Chapter 14 - Aunt Jennifer's Tigers (Adrienne Rich)

Q1 Who is the author of "Aunt Jennifer's Tigers"?
a. Emily Dickinson
b. Adrienne Rich
c. Maya Angelou
d. Sylvia Plath
Answer b. Adrienne Rich

Q2 The poem primarily explores the theme of
a. Love and relationships
b. Women's struggles and empowerment
c. Nature
d. Childhood
Answer b. Women's struggles and empowerment

Q3 What do Aunt Jennifer's tigers represent?
a. Weakness
b. Strength and independence
c. Fear
d. Domesticity
Answer b. Strength and independence

Q4 How does Aunt Jennifer create her tigers?
a. Through paintings
b. Through embroidery
c. Through sculptures
d. Through drawings
Answer b. Through embroidery

Q5 The act of stitching in the poem symbolizes
a. Freedom
b. Constraints of marriage
c. Joy
d. Indifference
Answer b. Constraints of marriage

Q6 How does Aunt Jennifer feel about her marriage?
a. Empowered
b. Trapped
c. Happy
d. Indifferent
Answer b. Trapped

Q7 The poem highlights the contrast between
a. Men and women
b. Strength and weakness
c. Art and reality
d. Youth and age
Answer b. Strength and weakness

Q8 The imagery used to describe the tigers suggests that they are
a. Timid
b. Strong and fierce
c. Indifferent
d. Lazy
Answer b. Strong and fierce

Q9 What does Aunt Jennifer wish for in her art?
a. To escape her reality
b. To showcase her happiness
c. To remain silent
d. To reflect her struggles
**Answer a. To escape her reality

Q10 The poem reflects on the limitations placed on women by
a. Society
b. Nature
c. Art
d. Family
Answer a. Society

Q11 What does Aunt Jennifer's heavy hands symbolize?
a. Freedom
b. Burden and oppression
c. Strength
d. Indifference
Answer b. Burden and oppression

Q12 How do the tigers behave in Aunt Jennifer's art?
a. Wild and fierce
b. Calm and gentle
c. Weak and timid
d. Indifferent
Answer a. Wild and fierce

Q13 The poem's tone can be described as
a. Joyful
b. Melancholic and reflective
c. Angry

d. Indifferent
Answer b. Melancholic and reflective

Q14 What does the conclusion of the poem suggest about Aunt Jennifer?
a. She is free
b. She remains oppressed
c. She has achieved her dreams
d. She is indifferent to her struggles
Answer b. She remains oppressed

Q15 The author uses the tigers to emphasize
a. The beauty of nature
b. The strength women can embody despite oppression
c. The insignificance of art
d. The futility of dreams
Answer b. The strength women can embody despite oppression

Q16 The poem ultimately conveys a message about
a. The need for art
b. The importance of individuality
c. Women's empowerment and the struggle against patriarchy
d. The significance of wealth
Answer c. Women's empowerment and the struggle against patriarchy

Q17 Aunt Jennifer's struggle is emblematic of
a. Personal challenges
b. Collective struggles of women
c. The joys of life
d. The importance of family
Answer b. Collective struggles of women

Q18 The overall message of "Aunt Jennifer's Tigers" suggests that
a. Women should remain silent
b. Women can find strength through creativity and art
c. Art is not important
d. Marriage is always fulfilling
Answer b. Women can find strength through creativity and art

Q19 How does the author illustrate Aunt Jennifer's character?
a. As weak and passive
b. As strong and vibrant
c. As conflicted and oppressed
d. As angry
Answer c. As conflicted and oppressed

Q20 The poem serves as a critique of
a. Artistic endeavors
b. Patriarchal structures
c. Nature
d. Education
Answer b. Patriarchal structures

Chapter 15 - The Third Level (Jack Finney)

Q1 Who is the author of "The Third Level"?
a. Jack Finney
b. John Updike
c. Kurt Vonnegut
d. Ray Bradbury
Answer a. Jack Finney

Q2 What is the main setting of the story?
a. A city
b. A train station
c. A library
d. A school
Answer b. A train station

Q3 The protagonist, Charley, discovers a third level at the train station that represents
a. The future
b. A different time period
c. His childhood
d. His dreams
Answer b. A different time period

Q4 What time period does Charley find himself in when he goes to the third level?
a. The 1920s
b. The 1950s
c. The 1940s
d. The 1890s
Answer d. The 1890s

Q5 How does Charley feel when he first discovers the third level?
a. Confused
b. Excited
c. Scared
d. Indifferent
Answer b. Excited

Q6 What does the third level symbolize in the story?
a. The past
b. Escape from reality
c. A dream
d. Imagination
Answer b. Escape from reality

Q7 What does Charley's wife, Louisa, think about his experiences?
a. She believes him
b. She thinks he is imagining things
c. She is excited
d. She is indifferent
Answer b. She thinks he is imagining things

Q8 The idea of the third level reflects Charley's desire for
a. Adventure
b. Simplicity and peace
c. Wealth
d. Knowledge
Answer b. Simplicity and peace

Q9 What does Charley attempt to do in the third level?
a. Buy tickets
b. Live a different life
c. Find his friends
d. Escape from his problems
Answer d. Escape from his problems

Q10 What literary device is prevalent in "The Third Level"?
a. Foreshadowing
b. Imagery
c. Symbolism
d. Irony
Answer c. Symbolism

Q11 What happens to Charley's friend, the psychiatrist, when he learns about the third level?
a. He believes Charley
b. He dismisses the idea
c. He becomes excited
d. He seeks to find the third level
Answer b. He dismisses the idea

Q12 How does the story conclude regarding Charley's experiences?
a. He finds the third level again
b. It is left ambiguous
c. He decides to leave reality
d. He realizes it was all a dream
Answer b. It is left ambiguous

Q13 What does Charley's journey to the third level represent about human nature?
a. The need for adventure
b. The desire to escape reality
c. The pursuit of happiness

d. The search for truth
Answer b. The desire to escape reality

Q14 The story's tone can be described as
a. Joyful
b. Nostalgic and contemplative
c. Angry
d. Indifferent
Answer b. Nostalgic and contemplative

Q15 What is the significance of the train station in the story?
a. It represents confusion
b. It symbolizes a transition
c. It is a place of danger
d. It is a place of comfort
Answer b. It symbolizes a transition

Q16 Charley's experiences in the third level ultimately reveal
a. The impossibility of escaping reality
b. The joy of living in the past
c. The beauty of imagination
d. The importance of friends
Answer a. The impossibility of escaping reality

Q17 The author uses vivid descriptions to depict
a. The chaos of the city
b. The serenity of the past
c. The beauty of nature
d. The excitement of trains
Answer b. The serenity of the past

Q18 How does Charley's character develop throughout the story?
a. He becomes more confused
b. He gains clarity about life
c. He becomes indifferent
d. He loses hope
Answer b. He gains clarity about life

Q19 What does the story suggest about the passage of time?
a. It is linear and unchanging
b. It is subjective and can be escaped
c. It is irrelevant
d. It should be feared
Answer b. It is subjective and can be escaped

Q20 The overall message of "The Third Level" reflects on
a. The beauty of the present
b. The desire to find peace in a chaotic world
c. The inevitability of change
d. The importance of tradition
Answer b. The desire to find peace in a chaotic world

Chapter 16 - The Tiger King (Kalki)

Q1 Who is the author of "The Tiger King"?
a. R. K. Narayan
b. Kalki
c. Kamala Das
d. Rabindranath Tagore
Answer b. Kalki

Q2 The story is set in which state of India?
a. Rajasthan
b. Maharashtra
c. Punjab
d. Uttar Pradesh
Answer a. Rajasthan

Q3 The protagonist of the story is
a. A tiger
b. A king
c. A hunter
d. A villager
Answer b. A king

Q4 What does the king aim to do to prove his bravery?
a. Hunt a tiger
b. Build a palace
c. Fight a war
d. Become wealthy
Answer a. Hunt a tiger

Q5 The story reflects on the theme of
a. Animal rights
b. The futility of pride and arrogance
c. The importance of tradition
d. The significance of wealth
Answer b. The futility of pride and arrogance

Q6 How does the king initially feel about his hunt for tigers?
a. Fearful
b. Confident
c. Indifferent
d. Sad
Answer b. Confident

Q7 The king's obsession with hunting leads to
a. A stronger kingdom
b. His downfall
c. Respect from his subjects
d. Increased wealth
Answer b. His downfall

Q8 The phrase "Tiger King" symbolizes
a. Strength and bravery
b. Fear and respect
c. Arrogance and foolishness
d. Wealth and power
Answer c. Arrogance and foolishness

Q9 The story conveys a message about
a. The importance of tradition
b. The respect for nature
c. The need for power
d. The role of kings
Answer b. The respect for nature

Q10 What is the king's ultimate fate in the story?
a. He becomes wealthy
b. He is defeated by a tiger
c. He is killed by a hunter
d. He dies of old age
Answer b. He is defeated by a tiger

Q11 The tone of the story can be described as
a. Serious
b. Humorous and satirical
c. Angry
d. Indifferent
Answer b. Humorous and satirical

Q12 The author uses irony to highlight the king's
a. Bravery
b. Foolishness
c. Intelligence
d. Kindness
Answer b. Foolishness

Q13 The king's attitude towards the tigers represents
a. Respect for animals
b. Greed and domination
c. Care for nature

d. Indifference
Answer b. Greed and domination

Q14 How does the king react to the news of a tiger sighting?
a. With joy
b. With fear
c. With anger
d. With indifference
Answer a. With joy

Q15 The character of the king can be best described as
a. Wise and kind
b. Arrogant and reckless
c. Humble and respectful
d. Indifferent and detached
Answer b. Arrogant and reckless

Q16 What lesson does the story ultimately teach about power?
a. It is necessary for control
b. It leads to arrogance and downfall
c. It should be cherished
d. It is irrelevant
Answer b. It leads to arrogance and downfall

Q17 The interactions between the king and his subjects highlight
a. Friendship
b. Conflict
c. Respect
d. Authority and fear
Answer d. Authority and fear

Q18 The story emphasizes the consequences of
a. Hunting
b. Wealth
c. Pride and arrogance
d. Education
Answer c. Pride and arrogance

Q19 What does the king's hunt for tigers reflect about human behavior?
a. The importance of coexistence
b. The desire for domination and control
c. The need for peace
d. The joy of nature
Answer b. The desire for domination and control

Q20 "The Tiger King" serves as a critique of
a. Tradition
b. Wildlife conservation
c. Colonialism
d. Human arrogance and greed
Answer d. Human arrogance and greed

Chapter 17 - Journey to the End of the Earth (Tishani Doshi)

Q1 Who is the author of "Journey to the End of the Earth"?
a. Tishani Doshi
b. Kamala Das
c. R. K. Narayan
d. Vikram Seth
Answer a. Tishani Doshi

Q2 The poem reflects on a journey to
a. The Arctic
b. The Antarctic
c. The Himalayas
d. The Sahara
Answer b. The Antarctic

Q3 The primary theme of the poem is
a. Adventure
b. Environmental consciousness
c. Fear
d. Wealth
Answer b. Environmental consciousness

Q4 The author's journey emphasizes the fragility of
a. Wildlife
b. Human life
c. Nature and ecosystems
d. Technology
Answer c. Nature and ecosystems

Q5 What is the significance of the title "Journey to the End of the Earth"?
a. It symbolizes a quest for knowledge
b. It represents the end of civilization
c. It highlights the beauty of the planet
d. It suggests a physical and metaphorical journey
Answer d. It suggests a physical and metaphorical journey

Q6 The poet uses vivid imagery to describe
a. Urban landscapes
b. The harsh conditions of Antarctica
c. The beauty of forests
d. The chaos of city life
Answer b. The harsh conditions of Antarctica

Q7 The journey serves as a reminder of
a. The importance of adventure
b. The consequences of human actions on the environment
c. The joy of exploration
d. The value of technology
Answer b. The consequences of human actions on the environment

Q8 What does the author discover about the Antarctic ecosystem?
a. It is thriving
b. It is endangered
c. It is irrelevant
d. It is unchanging
Answer b. It is endangered

Q9 The narrative reflects on the theme of
a. Human resilience
b. The insignificance of nature
c. Environmental responsibility
d. Adventure and exploration
Answer c. Environmental responsibility

Q10 The poet's experience in Antarctica evokes feelings of
a. Happiness
b. Anger
c. Awe and respect for nature
d. Indifference
Answer c. Awe and respect for nature

Q11 The imagery of the icy landscape symbolizes
a. Desolation and beauty
b. Danger and fear
c. Indifference
d. Warmth and comfort
Answer a. Desolation and beauty

Q12 What is the impact of climate change on the Antarctic environment, as discussed in the poem?
a. It is beneficial
b. It is harmful and destructive
c. It has no impact
d. It is reversible
Answer b. It is harmful and destructive

Q13 The journey represents a broader commentary on
a. The importance of travel
b. The need for human connection

c. The relationship between humans and nature
d. The significance of exploration
Answer c. The relationship between humans and nature

Q14 The tone of the poem can be described as
a. Light-hearted
b. Reflective and serious
c. Indifferent
d. Joyful
Answer b. Reflective and serious

Q15 How does the poet express her love for nature?
a. By describing its beauty and power
b. By ignoring its importance
c. By focusing on human achievements
d. By showing indifference
Answer a. By describing its beauty and power

Q16 What does the author encourage readers to do through her journey?
a. To travel to Antarctica
b. To appreciate nature and act responsibly
c. To avoid environmental issues
d. To seek adventure
Answer b. To appreciate nature and act responsibly

Q17 The overall message of "Journey to the End of the Earth" reflects on
a. The joy of travel
b. The importance of protecting the environment
c. The insignificance of human actions
d. The beauty of exploration
Answer b. The importance of protecting the environment

Q18 What does the journey reveal about human beings' place in nature?
a. They are dominant
b. They are insignificant
c. They are connected and responsible
d. They are indifferent
Answer c. They are connected and responsible

Q19 The poem encourages readers to
a. Ignore environmental issues
b. Appreciate the natural world
c. Seek wealth
d. Focus on urban life
Answer b. Appreciate the natural world

Q20 The journey serves as a metaphor for
a. The search for knowledge
b. The quest for environmental awareness
c. The pursuit of happiness
d. The need for competition
Answer b. The quest for environmental awareness

Chapter 18 - The Enemy (Pearl S. Buck)

Q1 Who is the author of "The Enemy"?
a. Pearl S. Buck
b. John Steinbeck
c. Ernest Hemingway
d. F. Scott Fitzgerald
Answer a. Pearl S. Buck

Q2 The story revolves around the relationship between
a. A soldier and his enemy
b. A doctor and a patient
c. A farmer and his land
d. A mother and child
Answer b. A doctor and a patient

Q3 The protagonist of the story is
a. Dr. Sadao
b. A soldier
c. A patient
d. The narrator
Answer a. Dr. Sadao

Q4 What is the main conflict faced by Dr. Sadao?
a. His identity
b. His loyalty to his country versus his duty as a doctor
c. His financial struggles
d. His relationship with his wife
Answer b. His loyalty to his country versus his duty as a doctor

Q5 What does Dr. Sadao find washed up on the shore?
a. A boat
b. A wounded soldier
c. A treasure chest
d. A message in a bottle
Answer b. A wounded soldier

Q6 The soldier Dr. Sadao saves is from
a. Japan
b. America
c. The enemy country
d. China
Answer c. The enemy country

Q7 How does Dr. Sadao feel about treating the soldier?
a. Indifferent
b. Angry and resentful
c. Compassionate and conflicted
d. Joyful
Answer c. Compassionate and conflicted

Q8 What internal struggle does Dr. Sadao face throughout the story?
a. The struggle for wealth
b. The struggle between duty and morality
c. The struggle for power
d. The struggle with his identity
Answer b. The struggle between duty and morality

Q9 What does the story highlight about the nature of humanity?
a. It is selfish
b. It is compassionate and complex
c. It is ruthless
d. It is indifferent
Answer b. It is compassionate and complex

Q10 How does Dr. Sadao's wife react to the soldier?
a. She is supportive
b. She is angry
c. She is indifferent
d. She is afraid
Answer b. She is angry

Q11 The climax of the story occurs when
a. The soldier dies
b. Dr. Sadao decides to let the soldier go
c. Dr. Sadao performs surgery
d. The authorities arrive
Answer b. Dr. Sadao decides to let the soldier go

Q12 The story emphasizes the theme of
a. War
b. Loyalty
c. Compassion amidst conflict
d. Family
Answer c. Compassion amidst conflict

Q13 What does Dr. Sadao ultimately decide to do with the soldier?
a. Turn him in
b. Help him escape
c. Leave him to die

d. Report him to the authorities
Answer b. Help him escape

Q14 The author uses vivid descriptions to highlight
a. The horrors of war
b. The beauty of nature
c. The chaos of life
d. The medical procedures
Answer a. The horrors of war

Q15 How does the soldier represent the theme of the enemy?
a. As a personification of evil
b. As a reflection of fear and misunderstanding
c. As a friend
d. As a competitor
Answer b. As a reflection of fear and misunderstanding

Q16 The overall message of "The Enemy" can be interpreted as
a. The need for conflict
b. The importance of compassion in humanity
c. The value of loyalty to one's country
d. The irrelevance of war
Answer b. The importance of compassion in humanity

Q17 Dr. Sadao's character can be best described as
a. Indifferent
b. Compassionate and conflicted
c. Selfish
d. Ruthless
Answer b. Compassionate and conflicted

Q18 What does Pearl S. Buck aim to convey through Dr. Sadao's character?
a. The importance of success
b. The complexity of human emotions in wartime
c. The futility of love
d. The need for revenge
Answer b. The complexity of human emotions in wartime

Q19 The story illustrates the idea that true humanity is defined by
a. Wealth
b. Actions in the face of adversity
c. Success in career
d. Indifference to suffering
Answer b. Actions in the face of adversity

Q20 The ending of the story emphasizes
a. Hope and redemption
b. Despair and loss
c. Victory in war
d. Indifference to others
Answer a. Hope and redemption

Chapter 19 - Should Wizard Hit Mommy (John Updike)

Q1 Who is the author of "Should Wizard Hit Mommy"?
a. John Updike
b. Kurt Vonnegut
c. Ray Bradbury
d. Philip Roth
Answer a. John Updike

Q2 The story centers around a
a. Child's fantasy
b. Parent-child relationship
c. Love story
d. Friendship
Answer b. Parent-child relationship

Q3 The main characters in the story are
a. A father and his daughter
b. A mother and her son
c. A teacher and a student
d. A husband and wife
Answer a. A father and his daughter

Q4 What is the primary conflict in the story?
a. A magical creature
b. A decision about a story
c. A disagreement between parents
d. A childhood game
Answer b. A decision about a story

Q5 The protagonist, Jack, tells stories to his daughter about
a. A wizard
b. A knight
c. A princess
d. A dragon
Answer a. A wizard

Q6 The story highlights the theme of
a. Innocence and imagination
b. Reality versus fantasy
c. Family dynamics
d. The importance of education
Answer c. Family dynamics

Q7 How does the daughter, Judy, react to the story?
a. With enthusiasm
b. With indifference
c. With anger
d. With confusion
Answer d. With confusion

Q8 What moral dilemma does Jack face while telling the story?
a. Whether to include magic
b. Whether to hit the mother character
c. Whether to change the ending
d. Whether to tell the story at all
Answer b. Whether to hit the mother character

Q9 The story reflects on the complexities of
a. Childhood fantasies
b. Parental expectations
c. Family traditions
d. Societal norms
Answer b. Parental expectations

Q10 What does Jack's storytelling symbolize?
a. His creativity
b. His authority as a parent
c. His failure as a father
d. His desire for freedom
Answer b. His authority as a parent

Q11 The tone of the story can be described as
a. Light-hearted
b. Serious and reflective
c. Humorous
d. Indifferent
Answer b. Serious and reflective

Q12 How does Jack feel about his storytelling abilities?
a. Confident
b. Insecure
c. Proud
d. Indifferent
Answer b. Insecure

Q13 The conflict between Jack and Judy illustrates
a. The generation gap
b. The joys of childhood
c. The importance of education

d. The need for adventure
Answer a. The generation gap

Q14 What does the ending of the story suggest about Jack's relationship with his daughter?
a. It is strong and unbreakable
b. It is strained and complicated
c. It is perfect
d. It is irrelevant
Answer b. It is strained and complicated

Q15 The character of Judy represents
a. The innocence of childhood
b. The complexity of growing up
c. The need for approval
d. The desire for adventure
Answer b. The complexity of growing up

Q16 Jack's internal conflict reflects the struggles of
a. Parent-child relationships
b. Childhood dreams
c. Societal expectations
d. Educational values
Answer a. Parent-child relationships

Q17 The story emphasizes the importance of
a. Tradition
b. Communication between parents and children
c. Wealth
d. Knowledge
Answer b. Communication between parents and children

Q18 The narrative ultimately critiques
a. Parental authority
b. Childlike innocence
c. Societal norms
d. Education systems
Answer a. Parental authority

Q19 What does Jack's character reveal about the struggles of parenthood?
a. It is easy and straightforward
b. It requires constant adjustment and understanding
c. It is irrelevant
d. It is fulfilling without challenges
Answer b. It requires constant adjustment and understanding

Q20 "Should Wizard Hit Mommy" illustrates the complexities of
a. Childhood fantasies
b. Family dynamics and communication
c. The pursuit of knowledge
d. Friendship
Answer b. Family dynamics and communication

Chapter 20 - On the Face of It (Susan Hill)

Q1 Who is the author of "On the Face of It"?
a. Susan Hill
b. John Steinbeck
c. Arthur Miller
d. J. D. Salinger
Answer a. Susan Hill.

Q2 The main characters in the play area
a. A teacher and a student
b. A mother and a daughter
c. A father and son
d. A grandfather and grandson
Answer a. A teacher and a student

Q3 What is the primary setting of the play?
a. A classroom
b. A park
c. A hospital
d. A home
Answer c. A hospital

Q4 The character of Mr Lamb is portrayed as
a. Bitter and angry
b. Kind and welcoming
c. Indifferent
d. Lonely
Answer b. Kind and welcoming

Q5 The play deals with the theme of
a. Friendship and connection
b. Wealth and status
c. Competition
d. Family dynamics
Answer a. Friendship and connection.

Q6 What does Derry struggle with throughout the play?
a. His financial situation
b. His physical appearance
c. His educational goals
d. His family life
Answer b. His physical appearance

Q7 The character of Derry can be best described as
a. Optimistic and cheerful
b. Angry and frustrated
c. Carefree and happy
d. Indifferent
Answer b. Angry and frustrated

Q8 What does Mr Lamb encourage Derry to do?
a. Stay away from others
b. Embrace life and accept himself
c. Hide from society
d. Ignore his problems
Answer b. Embrace life and accept himself

Q9 The play illustrates the importance of
a. Money
b. Relationships and understanding
c. Status
d. Power
Answer b. Relationships and understanding

Q10 The tone of the play can be described as
a. Light-hearted
b. Serious and reflective
c. Angry
d. Indifferent
Answer b. Serious and reflective

Q11 Derry's interactions with Mr Lamb reveal his
a. Indifference to others
b. Desire for acceptance and understanding
c. Need for wealth
d. Wish to escape reality
Answer b. Desire for acceptance and understanding

Q12 What does the wall symbolise in the play?
a. Separation
b. Protection
c. Freedom
d. Indifference
Answer a. Separation

Q13 The character of Mr Lamb represents
a. Society's expectations
b. Wisdom and compassion
c. Indifference

d. Wealth
Answer b. Wisdom and compassion

Q14 The play ultimately conveys a message about
a. The importance of wealth
b. The power of friendship and acceptance
c. The futility of life
d. The necessity of competition
Answer b. The power of friendship and acceptance

Q15 What does the play's ending suggest about Derry's character development?
a. He remains unchanged
b. He learns to embrace himself
c. He becomes more bitter
d. He decides to hide from the world
Answer b. He learns to embrace himself

Q16 The dialogue between Derry and Mr Lamb reflects the theme of
a. Family relationships
b. Human connection and understanding
c. Wealth and status
d. Education
Answer b. Human connection and understanding

Q17 The overall message of "On the Face of It" emphasises
a. The importance of superficiality
b. The significance of inner beauty and acceptance
c. The irrelevance of personal struggles
d. The necessity of competition
Answer b. The significance of inner beauty and acceptance

Q18 How does Mr Lamb's character influence Derry?
a. He brings negativity
b. He inspires hope and acceptance
c. He ignores Derry
d. He complicates Derry's life
Answer b. He inspires hope and acceptance

Q19 The author uses vivid imagery to depict
a. The beauty of nature
b. The struggles of human emotions
c. The chaos of life
d. The simplicity of daily life
Answer b. The struggles of human emotions

Q20 "On the Face of It" ultimately conveys that true acceptance comes from

a. Wealth

b. Inner strength and connection with others

c. Education

d. Success

Answer b. Inner strength and connection with others

Chapter 21 - Evans Tries an O-Level (Colin Dexter)

Q1 Who is the author of "Evans Tries an O-Level"?
a. Agatha Christie
b. Colin Dexter
c. Arthur Conan Doyle
d. Ian Fleming
Answer b. Colin Dexter

Q2 What is the primary setting of the story?
a. A school
b. A prison
c. A courtroom
d. A library
Answer b. A prison

Q3 The protagonist, Evans, is attempting to take an examination in
a. Mathematics
b. English
c. History
d. Geography
Answer b. English

Q4 What does Evans use to help him escape?
a. A map
b. A disguise
c. A vehicle
d. Money
Answer b. A disguise

Q5 The story revolves around the theme of
a. Deception and cleverness
b. Wealth and power
c. Education and knowledge
d. Friendship
Answer a. Deception and cleverness.

Q6 What is the primary conflict in the story?
a. A struggle for power
b. An escape from prison
c. A race against time
d. A personal vendetta
Answer b. An escape from prison

Q7 How does the story portray the character of Evans?
a. As foolish
b. As clever and resourceful
c. As arrogant
d. As indifferent
Answer b. As clever and resourceful

Q8 The tone of the story can be described as
a. Serious
b. Humorous and clever
c. Sad
d. Angry
Answer b. Humorous and clever

Q9 What is the role of the governor in the story?
a. He is indifferent
b. He is supportive of Evans
c. He is sceptical and cautious
d. He is ignorant
Answer c. He is sceptical and cautious

Q10 What does Evans' character reveal about human nature?
a. It is selfish
b. It is cunning and adaptable
c. It is naive
d. It is weak
Answer b. It is cunning and adaptable

Q11 What method does Evans use to communicate with the outside world?
a. Letters
b. A phone
c. Disguised calls
d. Secret messages
Answer c. Disguised calls

Q12 The story emphasises the importance of
a. Trust
b. Intelligence and quick thinking
c. Physical strength
d. Wealth
Answer b. Intelligence and quick thinking

Q13 How does the narrative create suspense?
a. By revealing the ending first
b. Through the use of vivid imagery
c. By gradually uncovering Evans' plan

d. By focusing on the governor’s doubts
Answer c. By gradually uncovering Evans' plan

Q14 What does the ending of the story reveal about Evans?
a. He is caught
b. He escapes successfully
c. He changes his mind
d. He surrenders
Answer b. He escapes successfully

Q15 The story illustrates the concept of
a. Loyalty
b. Education as a means of empowerment
c. Crime and punishment
d. Friendship
Answer b. Education as a means of empowerment

Q16 The character of the governor can be seen as a representation of
a: Authority
b. Ignorance
c. Kindness
d. Indifference
Answer a. Authority

Q17 Evans’ cleverness is highlighted through his ability to
a. Deceive those in power
b. Win arguments
c. Outsmart his friends
d. Escape from danger
Answer a. Deceive those in power.

Q18 The overall message of "Evans Tries an O-Level" emphasises
a. The futility of rebellion
b. The importance of intelligence in overcoming obstacles
c. The need for cooperation
d. The significance of wealth
Answer b. The importance of intelligence in overcoming obstacles

Q19 How does the author create a sense of irony in the story?
a. By making Evans a sympathetic character
b. By showcasing the incompetence of authority figures
c. By revealing the truth at the end
d. By contrasting Evans’ plan with reality
Answer b. By showcasing the incompetence of authority figures

Q20 The narrative ultimately challenges readers to reflect on
a. The nature of justice
b. The power of cleverness and determination
c. The significance of education
d. The consequences of crime
Answer b. The power of cleverness and determination

Chapter 22 - Memories of Childhood (Zitkala-Sa & Bama)

Q1 Who are the authors of "Memories of Childhood"?
a. R. K. Narayan and John Updike
b. Zitkala-Sa and Bama
c. Kamala Das and Emily Dickinson
d. Maya Angelou and Toni Morrison
Answer b. Zitkala-Sa and Bama

Q2 The narrative explores the theme of
a. Freedom and independence
b. Displacement and Identity
c. Adventure and exploration
d. Wealth and poverty
Answer b. Displacement and Identity

Q3 Zitkala-Sa's story reflects on her experiences as
a. A student in a boarding school
b. A teacher
c. A mother
d. A writer
Answer a. A student in a boarding school

Q4 Bama's narrative primarily focuses on her experiences as
a. A girl in a rural setting
b. A city dweller
c. A student in an urban school
d. A traveller
Answer a. A girl in a rural setting

Q5 What does Zitkala-Sa's experience in the boarding school symbolise?
a. The loss of cultural identity
b. The pursuit of knowledge
c. The joy of childhood
d. The beauty of friendship
Answer a. The loss of cultural identity

Q6 Bama's story emphasises the importance of
a. Wealth
b. Education
c. Family traditions
d. Cultural heritage
Answer d. Cultural heritage

Q7 The tone of Zitkala-Sa's narrative can be described as
a. Joyful
b. Nostalgic and reflective
c. Angry
d. Indifferent
Answer b. Nostalgic and reflective

Q8 Bama faces discrimination based on
a. Gender
b. Caste
c. Wealth
d. Education
Answer b. Caste

Q9 The interactions Zitkala-Sa has with her peers reflect.
a. Friendship
b. Hostility and exclusion
c. Acceptance
d. Indifference
Answer b. Hostility and exclusion

Q10 What is the primary conflict in Bama's narrative?
a. Struggles with family
b. The challenge of overcoming societal norms
c. The pursuit of education
d. Personal ambition
Answer b. The challenge of overcoming societal norms

Q11 Both narratives highlight the importance of
a. Wealth
b. Cultural identity
c. Individualism
d. Urbanization
Answer b. Cultural identity

Q12 What does Zitkala-Sa's story reveal about her relationship with her mother?
a. Indifference
b. Strong and supportive
c. Strained
d. Fearful
Answer b. Strong and supportive

Q13 The overall message of "Memories of Childhood" reflects on
a. The joy of childhood experiences
b. The complexities of cultural identity and social justice
c. The insignificance of personal struggles

d. The necessity of wealth
Answer b. The complexities of cultural identity and social justice

Q14 How do Zitkala-Sa and Bama's experiences differ?
a. They both face similar challenges
b. Their backgrounds and environments shape their experiences differently
c. They have no differences
d. They both live in urban settings
Answer b. Their backgrounds and environments shape their experiences differently

Q15 The stories encourage readers to reflect on
a. The importance of wealth
b. The significance of identity and culture
c. The joys of childhood
d. The need for competition
Answer b. The significance of identity and culture

Q16 The authors use vivid imagery to illustrate
a. The joy of childhood
b. The struggles faced by marginalised individuals
c. The beauty of nature
d. The excitement of adventure
Answer b. The struggles faced by marginalised individuals

Q17 How do the narratives challenge societal norms?
a. By ignoring them
b. By highlighting the need for change
c. By promoting wealth
d. By encouraging competition
Answer b. By highlighting the need for change

Q18 The tone of Bama's narrative can be described as
a. Angry and resentful
b. Joyful and celebratory
c. Reflective and critical
d. Indifferent
Answer c. Reflective and critical

Q19 What does the conclusion of the narratives suggest about childhood experiences?
a. They are unimportant
b. They shape one's identity and values
c. They should be forgotten
d. They are irrelevant
Answer b. They shape one's identity and values

Q20 "Memories of Childhood" ultimately conveys a message about
a. The joy of material wealth
b. The importance of understanding one's cultural roots and identity
c. The necessity of competition
d. The insignificance of childhood
Answer b. The importance of understanding one's cultural roots and identity